LIQUID LOVE

• One Woman's Spiritual Journey with Liquid Love • Explore Deeper and Greater Power Level • Meet And Advocate Sent from Your Designer and Hear How He Speaks • Read About an Unexplained Joy That Comes from Your Belly (John 7:38)

by Evangelist Sherry D. Nelson
Licensed & Ordained Minister of the Gospel Graduated of the University of Washington with Science Degree (BS) Also Graduate of the A. L. Hardy Academy of Theology with a Bachelor and Master's in Religion (BRE, MRE)

The contents of this work, including, but not limited to, the accuracy of events, people, and places depicted; opinions expressed; permission to use previously published materials included; and any advice given or actions advocated are solely the responsibility of the author, who assumes all liability for said work and indemnifies the publisher against any claims stemming from publication of the work.

Dorrance Publishing Co
585 Alpha Drive
Suite 103
Pittsburgh, PA 15238
Visit our website at *www.dorrancebookstore.com*

ISBN: 979-8-8868-3130-6
eISBN: 979-8-8868-3989-0

LIQUID LOVE

• One Woman's Spiritual Journey with Liquid Love • Explore Deeper and Greater Power Level • Meet And Advocate Sent from Your Designer and Hear How He Speaks • Read About an Unexplained Joy That Comes from Your Belly (John 7:38)

The Favor You Did Not Know

A new love level, a true story, a real experience, and a burst of love. A new revelation of power. We may be living beneath our favor privilege, get more privilege, or have the power to produce love for the kingdom and others. Consider the warnings against living on "milk and not meat." There is a power baptism available. (Isaiah 4:4 Acts 1:5 Matt. 3:11 Luke 3:16)

Knowing is not enough. Simply knowing the principles is not enough. Principles not applied are weak. They can lead to being alone. (James 2:17, 2:14, 2:26, Gal. 5:6) An Advocate is assigned as the comforter specifically to you, His children from the son. The comforter has come to teach a firm love foundation that is strengthened; we have a Holy Spirit teacher when we submit and surrender: a supernatural surgery, a spiritual operation from God. (John 14:15, 16, 17, 18)

Operations of the comforter demonstrate a divine advocate in the life of a girl named Linda. Linda yields to the advocate, comforter, and teacher in everyday life situations. She allowed the greater love to operate. She submitted to the greater love.

You have the opportunity to build yourself up on your most holy faith by speaking in tongues often. Here is a look into situations where God gets the glory. Liquid love is a promotion, a supernatural promotion into power, and it included soaking up the love from the Holy Spirit to saturate and absorb the Love from the Holy Spirit. It is God's third baptism for the saints.

Love to share is all given by the Spirit of God with the different gifts from Jesus through different gifts, different administrations, and different manifestations of gifts. (I Cor. 12:1-14) Love is given for the power work of the ministry in the earth. (The harvest is plenty, but the labors are few.) Discover the evidence of speaking in tongues to proclaim that the baptism is complete. The more you speak in tongues, the more you empower your will for Jesus Christ.

Supernatural Food Bank

You cannot give what you do not have. When your love bank is love low, you have nothing to draw from. God is love. Love is of God.

God is love < Jesus First.
High Revenue
Lots of Love

God is love. Love is a person (supernatural holy person). He will help you do right when you want to do wrong. Linda felt the liquid love. She felt the presence of the Lord. She knew she was never alone, and through every situation, she could call on Jesus and His liquid love, He was not far, just a whisper away. "Help me, Jesus," was just a breath away. The liquid love of Jesus gave her more faith, more courage, and it reduced the enemy attack. She could see them coming, and she kept the sword of the Spirit in her mind and heart more often. Often, God would prepare her in advance of the attack. The storms of life will come, but God will help us through when our mind stays on Him.

Just like God changed the disciples in the scriptures, He will change us to see the supernatural, feel the invisible, and hear the unspoken. Linda felt the invisible (water), saw the supernatural (clouds), and her ears were unstopped and cleared out to hear the unspoken. God gave her a new power to use directly from Jesus Christ with the evidence of speaking in an unknown tongue.

The Holy Ghost Baptism Gifts (II Corinthians 12: 1-11) are gifts to glorify God to do a greater work and to build His kingdom. We must worship God and not His gifts. The Holy Spirit comes to live inside us. He is a peacemaker who is like a pacemaker in your heart. He works directly inside to set the Jesus-pacemaker heart to help you keep your focus and direction on Jesus and the things of God. He is the Holy Pacemaker for the body of Christ. He keeps the heart healthy towards Jesus.

A Position, A Purpose, and a Power Assignment

Linda had a desire in her heart to pour out more love on her family and friends. Her faith increased as she continued in Bible school at the Christian Academy. Her first step was that she went to missionary classes, then she continued to the BRE class (bible of religious education. She already had a Bachelor of science degree in speech pathology (emotional and physical speech restoration application in the school of communication) from a university. She was accelerated in the BRE classes. The Bible class gave her an anchor in God's word, an anchor of understanding of the bible (if it had not been for this, she surely would have been a train wreck).

Linda was a newlywed for the most part, only married one year now and attending a new church with her husband. Her now husband had asked her to quit her job as a teacher at a center teaching reading and comprehension skills to trade applicants who were mostly male students. She loved her job working at a pre-vocational center class for carpentry, automotive, culinary, electrical, and plumbing. However, she decided to be a good wife and make her husband happy, so she quit, gave notice, and got married. After all, her husband to be had a good job with a big company and good pay. Later she found out it was a "control issue" he had that was his real reason.

2

No Problem

Her husband encouraged her to attend Bible school at his church and had no problem with that. Linda enjoyed the Bible already because she had been an active member at her own church, especially after her supernatural experience with God just a year earlier. She was eager to learn what had really happen to her and what the Bible had to say about it.

The marriage failed due to infidelity on his part. But the word of God and the Bible school compelled her to stay in classes. The teachings were an anchor she could hold onto. God's word would keep her afloat through the storms: all the infidelity, turmoil, headaches, and pain. She would survive his mistakes, her mistakes, his meanness, and her meanness. Through it all, God never left her by herself, and she still had her faith in God. Linda did not believe in divorce; her parents were a beautiful picture of what love is supposed to look like.

Linda was now ashamed, disappointed, defeated, and in a state cognitive dissonance, despair, and a feeling of bitterness while in the midst of all the turmoil. She made some poor decisions and sought revenge. But God was patient and kind and taught her how to forgive herself first then the situation.

She continued in bible school, and even with her poor choices, she was still faithful to her studies. She learned that feeling sorry for herself would be a death sentence. God let her know when you repent, there is no problem. When she repented, she learned God had her back, so she changed her attitude to line up with the Bible. Linda felt like the enemy wanted to take her out because the Lord must really have a serious plan for her life. Linda learned that life can hurt but God knows how to heal. A total healing requires forgiveness for all involved.

She had to admit she had wanted a husband, he was older and in the church, but he was not really a great choice. She wanted help raising her two teen children. She never dreamed he would be a cheater as he seemed a safe choice. She was now delivered, wounded but delivered from her past. Now, she knew people cannot make us happy but we must be content in Jesus and he will give us joy. Happiness is temporal and temporary. But Joy is eternal and everlasting.

The foundation of all love and happiness is God. All love requires a foundation. Linda learns this liquid love is beginning to pour out through her onto others. The liquid love is holding Linda together, the liquid love is showing Linda how not to be selfish about all her own mistakes, and it is helping Linda from becoming a bitter person. The love of Jesus does cover a multitude of faults; in retrospect, she was comforted at the heart level and convinced that forgiveness is a gift from God and not of ourselves.

Miracle Ears

She was not sure what happened or how she got on the floor. She did not feel a fall and she was not hurt anywhere. One thing she knew for sure is that she was on the floor laying on her back. Her arms were stretched out, and she remembered her ears had popped open and water shot out of her ears just like a hose under pressure. Now, she was laying on the floor in a pool of water from her head to her feet. Just like you pop a bottle of wine, and the cork pops and wine shoots out. Her eyes open. She is on the floor and she feels the wet water. She is laying in a pool of water.

She thought, "What happened?" She feels the water with her hand to make sure it was water. She says again to herself, "Yes this is water, let me get up from here on this floor in a pool of water." She hears someone standing over her. She reaches up to get off the floor. She sees her pastor standing over her to lift her up. He takes her hand and helps lift her up.

Her natural observation is that she is not wet, nor are her clothes or hands. She remembers coming to the front of the church when the pastor said to come to the front if you wish to be baptized in the Holy Spirit. Standing there together with her pastor in the front of the church was very foggy and cloudy. She looked around, and sure enough, there was a white misty cloud in the whole church.

She looks up, and the cloud is more concentrated over her head. She looks up and she hears herself speak in an unknown language. Her voice has a new language, and she could now see the soundwaves going up in a straight vertical line up to the cloud. She keeps looking at these sound waves going into the cloud up to the ceiling. The white concentrated cloud is taking her voice up, and she can see the frequency in the air like blue light directly into the misty clouds. She stands observing the whole thing. Just standing there looking up, it was just like a movie. A silent movie all so clear. The only thing is, she is the character. Then, it is time to break the silence and the slow-motion movie and the sound waves she can see. She hears her pastor say, "You got it, you got it." These words woke her up and seemed to bring her concentration back to her natural reality. She stopped looking up, and she stopped speaking. She looked at her pastor, he was smiling and seemed very happy. He gave her a hug and she went back to her seat in the church. She went back to her seat and sat there replaying the whole thing in her mind.

She was not sure what all happened and what it all meant, but she knew she had an experience with God, a supernatural experience. She would later understand that this was the Supernatural Baptism in the Holy Spirit. Linda knew she had been in the floor, laying on her back, and she was lying in a shallow pool of water, maybe a couple of gallons, from the crown of her head to the sole of her feet.

It felt like water, it felt wet laying there, and she touched it with her hands. She knew it came out of her ears because she was aware that both her ears shot out a fountain of water. It seemed her ears had corks that popped out of both ears and the water gushed out. Both ears at the same time were a fountain of water. She stopped and she could feel that it was wet on the floor. She did not feel the fall, but she felt the water fountains with no pain. She felt the water with her body and hands. But when she stood up with the help of the pastor, she was not wet. Later, she concluded that she must've been in supernatural water and had a supernatural fall.

Her supernatural experience let her see and hear the sound waves of her voice, and she knew then that God had to be in the cloud. (She understood that she was in the presence of God in the cloud and the misty room.) The sound waves were real, and she could see them as they floated up in the white cloud spotlight that was shining directly on her.

The Spotlight of Clouds

She saw the spotlight of clouds, and the voice frequency waves that floated above her were clear. Back at her seat, she sat and pondered what this all meant. Linda knew and believed at this time she was truly baptized in the Holy Ghost just like the people in the book of Acts. This was what her preacher/pastor had explained that night in the sermon. But who could she tell this to? This was different. These Baptist people might not believe what she says. This is the first time she heard a Baptist preacher preach on the baptism in the Holy Spirit.

Linda remembered her sister saying, "They are Pentecostal" (her church she attended seemed a little strange). Her sister tried to tell her a lot of stuff she said was in the Bible that her Baptist folk did not teach. So, Linda asked God; she said, "God, I do not want to get involved in any strange religious teaching I never heard about." Linda found out God really would speak to her after she asked Him.

Sitting in morning worship at church, her pastor said, "Tonight I will be teaching on the baptism into the Holy Spirit."

Linda thought in her heart, "Too bad I will not be back tonight, you should have preached it this morning, I will not be in back to the seven P.M. service." Then, she heard a voice as clear as a bell in her spirit, "You asked me, didn't you?" Linda knew it was God. She knew she had to come back to the night service to hear what she needed to know about the baptism of the Holy Spirit. One thing Linda learned later is that there is more than one baptism; there are three:

One into the body of Christ, drawn by the Holy Spirit

One in natural water, ordinance by the pastor of the church

One into the baptism of the Holy Spirit, Supernatural water performed by Jesus Christ

She sat there in the church remembering what she had told God in her heart. "I love my sister, but she did not plan to trust her sister's belief over what she thought God wanted for her and for her to do." Linda was reminded that she had prayed in her heart. "Lord if there is something else you want me to know, you will have to tell me yourself."

The Lord did speak to her spirit and answered her prayer by a supernatural experience, the baptism in the Holy Spirit that he revealed, and this experience is available to all believers after they have received the first two baptisms from God

1. *Baptism into salvation-the body of Christ by faith and the belief (inward experience)*
2. *Baptism in water by the preacher-outward show*

3. *Baptism into the Holy Ghost by Jesus Christ*

God is so good. Later, she would learn more about this personal experience of baptism into the Holy Spirit. The fall was her emergence into the Holy Spirit. The spoken new language was evidence of the spirit that dwelled inside. The cloud was the presence of the Lord.

Holy Water for Baptism (Supernatural Spirit)

She was wet from her head down to her feet. It felt like water, but not natural water, supernatural water. Lord, what does all this mean? She needed knowledge and understanding in His bible. God said He would give His knowledge and understanding. After church, she knew all the questions had not been answered (but her sister was right). God did have something different for her in the Holy Spirit. Would her ears hear better now? All that water that flowed like a fountain out of both ears. A serious fountain shower of water, supernatural water. Will she see better now? God, He gave her eyes to see the supernatural and the cloud of "Shekinah glory." Like the Glory of God, the cloud is like the one that entered the temple in 2 Chronicles 7:14.

She had these questions:

1. *Will she read God's word through a supernatural lens?*
2. *Will she hear the hearts of men? The unspoken word? Can she pray now different with a new language that goes behind the obvious need?*
3. *Will her new language of prayer attack the enemy forces?*

4. *Will her faith have more supernatural foundation?*

5. *Will the relationship she has with God grow?*

6. *Has Jesus Christ's favor and relationship increased?*

The Lord feels closer. Questions, questions, does the Lord have a new vision and a new assignment in His Church? Questions, questions, she feels confident the Lord will answer soon. She steps out of the church onto the porch outside of the sanctuary right outside the double doors.

She investigates the clear night sky. The porchlight is on, but the sky looks extra clear as the moon is full, and the air is fresh and clear. She notices the world seems to speak to her. The Fall moon, the great clear night, the trees so green, and the hanging quiet. No one is on the porch but her. The trees and the sky seem to come in very close, larger than natural. She looks at herself through new eyes, and it seems her frame is so much smaller.

She looks like a little doll standing on the church porch. The porch is so small and the church a doll house. The sky is looking particularly blue with all the different shades of blue, bright, light blue, soft blues, bordered by the dark night blues. She thinks to herself, "Wow, the Earth is large, and I am so small. God is so big, and I am so small, just like a tiny doll, only a finger size of a person, beside God. I think I see God," she thought. "I am so small; this is God's Earth."

People come out of the church and she goes home. She ponders all this in her heart. This was the night she saw God, the night her eyes could see the real measure of her existence. Her eyes saw God. The Earth is the Lord's. Her eyes saw her tiny self and her own need of GOD, how tiny we are, and how God still cares about such a tiny person. And how giant his love is for us. He is a giant in our world, and we are but a speck in His world. The comfort of God overflowed through her that night. His love and protection were evident.

Linda felt safe by God's great love. She told no one. A couple of years later, she got married. She left that assembly and never heard another message at that church about the baptism into the Holy Ghost. She married a church member and started Bible class in the missionary class, still pondering all that had happened to her and how God spoke to her. The marriage was unsuccessful, but she remained at the church and in the Bible school ran by the Pastor. The pastor at the Bible School answered a lot of her questions regarding her Holy Ghost and supernatural experience.

The new pastor's favorite chapter of the Bible seemed to be the book of Acts, where the disciples, Peter in particular, received power after he was baptized into the Holy Spirit. Linda went through many storms and hurricanes from the enemy. It seems the enemy had her on the hitlist to take her out and her influences in the Kingdom of God. Her marriage ended in divorce.

Staying in Bible school in a church where her ex-husband attended and remarried himself, she finished missionary school with a bachelor's and master's degree. Through it all, God had taught Linda how to pray in the Spirit, which is the Holy Spirit, praying in tongues, praying in victory, and praying directly to God by the Spirit of God. (Jesus baptizes His saints for the work of the ministry to build them up in power). The enemy, Satan, comes to kill, steal, and destroy your influence in the kingdom of God.

Speaking in tongues is a weapon in this warfare. It is by the Spirit of God that builds up your spirit to overcome the attack of the enemy. Linda remembered the night she fell out on the floor in front of the church. Both ears at the same time popped and flooded out water on the floor. She did not feel the fall and when she stood up (someone helped her). The white cloud in the room was very clear. She saw it when she looked up at the white cloud over her.

She began to speak in a foreign language. She stood there watching the sound waves go up to the cloud. The sound waves were real, and she could see them as they floated up to the cloud. She asked herself, "What does this all mean? Who can I tell this all to? God is doing something to me. I know it is God." She is reminded of the conversation with her sister. She attended a Pentecostal Church and shared a lot of strange occurrences.

She loved her sister but would not subscribe to all her beliefs, one of which was, "We could have a Holy Spirit's power where we speak in an unknown tongue." It seems like in every conversation we would have that would always come up. Then one day, she was getting on Linda's last nerve. Linda thought to herself, "Did Linda tell God from her heart? I love my sister, but I do not plan to trust her belief over what God wanted me to do." She said in her heart (your heart knows how to pray). I do not want to do anything against you, God. I had never heard a sermon on "speaking in tongues," and I know the Holy Spirit gave him a special joy.

Sometimes when the pastor got extra excited, he jumped around the pulpit while he was preaching. "Lord, my pastor now has not preached on personal Holy Ghost power, so whatever Faye is talking about, I do not believe. Lord, if there is something else you want me to know, you will have to tell me yourself."

Sitting in the pew, the whole situation unfolded. She is reminded of the bad dreams. The dreams of the dark shadow. The shadow of a man that saying, "Don't speak. Don't speak in a threatening way." A confusing dream, she is not sure what "don't speak" means. "Speak about what?" She was reminded that her pastor, David Hardy Sr., had said in morning worship. "Tonight I will be preaching on the baptism in the Holy Spirit in the books of Acts."

This is where you speak in tongues. She spoke to herself in a mocking tone, "Well, you should have preached it this morning at 11 A.M. service, I do not plan to come back to the 7 P.M. service tonight." (She never attended the night service.) Sitting in her seat in morning worship, she heard a voice. She knew it was the Lord. He said, "You asked me about it, didn't you?" She did ask the Lord and he was going to tell her the truth at 7 P.M. night service at the church.

This was God speaking so she knew she had to come back. Her pastor preached the sermon out of the book of Acts. Then she heard her pastor say, "All who want the baptism into the Holy Ghost come forward to receive more power, come forward to the front to receive from the Lord." She got up out of her seat and went to the front of the church to pray with her pastor. She remembered him praying and reaching to lay hands on her head. She did not feel anything after that until she woke up on the floor.

Then, she saw and heard everything. She saw the water. She saw she was on the floor. She saw the cloud. She saw the sound waves go up into the cloud from her own voice. She heard the people speak. She heard the foreign language come out of her own voice. She sat and re-played the whole situation in her mind. It was all a supernatural experience.

The fall was not felt.

The water was not wet.

Linda saw the cloud was God's presence.

The spoken language was never learned by Linda.

*A Holy language to surrender to God was real, Linda
now knew.*

Linda knew the Baptism of the Holy Spirit, an emergence down in the spirit of God for herself. She was laying down on the floor in The Supernatural Holy Spirit water. When she stood up, she was not wet. She fell in the water, not natural water, but Supernatural Holy water.

Linda Remembers the Night
The Sky Experience

Standing on the church porch, Linda looked up into the clear blue sky of the night. The sky was so clear the porch light was on, but the sky was so over-powering. The sky seemed to come down to the porch, and the moon was extra bright. The greenery of the trees seemed to have a comfortable touch. It was almost as if Linda saw God, and his awesome big creation seemed to give her a hug. The blue sky seemed close enough to touch. Her eyes were fixed on the covering of the clean, fresh smell of the night air.

The sky seemed close enough to almost touch and was bordered by the green trees. It appears she was in the hands of God. Linda will never forget that night. She thought to herself, "I see God." The sky came in so close. She was just a tiny doll as she looked at herself and felt His divine protection all around her. She had a divine feeling of comfort and power and protection. Linda looked away after a few minutes away from the sky, and her mind brought her back to her natural size, and it seemed the sky moved away to its normal vision field. A joy welled up in Linda.

Someone came out of the church onto the porch. She thought to herself," God is nearer to me that ever before." She had a secret, she was allowed a greater glimpse into God and His power. Through his creation, He had let her "see Him." Her heart was filled with extra joy. She remembers the scripture after some years. The experience in relationship to the scripture that says, "The Earth is the Lord's and the fullness thereof the world and they that dwell therein. He was founded it up on the seas and established it among the floods."

This big Earth belongs to God and is created by Him. People get it twisted and worship the Earth rather than the God who made the Earth. Worshipping the creation rather than the creator, the one who designed it all. She wanted to tell everyone in the church, "I saw God, he let me see His presence and He let me see my tiny self in relation to his big Earth just as a tiny girl."

His love was so present she could feel it in the clear quiet breeze in the air as she was compelled to look up into the sky. But who would believe her? So, she went to the car and went home. She knew it was the new sermon her Pastor preached. She knew it was God who had compelled the new pastor to preach on the subject of how the converts were baptized and spoke in tongues (strange languages) on the Day of Pentecost. Pentecost means fifty days after Jesus rose from the dead, fifty days after Jews became a Nation of People, Pentecost means fifty.

Linda believed that God speaks to ordinary people, but it was the first time she experienced His presence like this. So, she pondered this all in her heart-and kept it to herself. Though she did begin to practice speaking in tongues, she would pray and sometimes sing in an unknown tongue. She was gaining more confidence to use her gift as the spirit of God would allow. Speaking in tongues seemed to build up her spirit.

A few years later, she married a man from a Pentecostal church and started Bible School. The marriage failed miserably but Linda stayed close to God and kept her language alive and flowing as she learned from Bible School. She studied to understand the scriptures regarding her new gift of tongues and what the Bible had says about. She learned all nine gifts are available after the supernatural third baptism into the holy Spirit according to 1 Corinthians 12:1-11.

Supernatural Gifts for the Saints (born again believers of Jesus Christ) They are all operated by the one Holy Spirit - the Spirit of God

1. *Supernatural Word of Wisdom*
2. *Supernatural Word of Knowledge*
3. *Supernatural Diverse (many) Kinds of Tongues*
4. *Supernatural Faith*
5. *Supernatural Healings*
6. *Supernatural Workings of Miracles*
7. *Supernatural Prophecy – (foretell things to come)*
8. *Supernatural Discerning of the Spirit (whether they are of God)*
9. *Supernatural Interpretation of Tongues - (When one speaks in prophecy the message explained)*

The Holy Spirit of God is the operator. The one same Spirit runs operations for all these gifts. There are many operations but one Holy Spirit operates them all. The enemy (Satan) might try to copy, but our God says always check in with Him. Scripture says try the spirits, whether they be of God, whether they be of the Holy Spirit of God. I Corinthians 12:13, For by one Holy Spirit we are all baptized into the body of Christ.

The Body Of Christ His Church

> *One body but many members (people – titles - many members)*
>
> *One body many members (purpose supernatural operations)*
>
> *One body many administrations (positions and ordinances)*
>
> *Apostles, Prophets, Pastors, Teachers*
>
> *Workers of Miracles*
>
> *Workers of Healings*
>
> *Workers of Helps*
>
> *Holy Government Positions*
>
> *Diversities (many) Tongues – power gift*

The gift of salvation where you accept the birth, the death, the burial, and the resurrection of Jesus Christ, you are now a baptized believer into the Body of Jesus Christ. Romans 10:9

The Word of Wisdom Mark 11:23,24, tells what to do with the supernatural knowledge over a situation. In the Word of Knowledge, God reveals supernatural information unknown to you previously. The Gift of Faith is no doubt a supernatural faith, a belief for big things.

Gifts of Healing are to speak the words of power to be made whole, a compelled way to pray for a sick person from the Holy Spirit. Working of Miracles is when God does the work by your hand (God is in operation through the saint and the miracle is performed to the glory of God). The Gift of Prophecy is for comfort, prophecy confirms a word from the Lord. Gift of Discernment is the knowledge of which spirit is in operation (human spirit, spirit of God, devil spirit) and confirms what spirit is in operation, good or bad.

Who Is The Holy Spirit and How Does He Operate?

The Holy Spirit is our helper and our guide. No God thing will He withhold from them who seek Him. He will keep our hearts and mind in perfect peace when we lean on Him. The Holy Spirit is sent from Jesus Christ to be our comforter. He is our comforter (I John 4:26, 27) our personal advocate, the spirit who speaks only of Jesus Christ and teaches God's children how to serve and grow in the grace and knowledge of Jesus Christ. Linda was reminded the first time she was tested by the enemy after she had recently received the Holy Spirit baptism.

The Second Experience

She was still trying to figure out what had happened to her and understand the transformation in her own spirit and how this extra experience according to the book of Acts 2:1-4 would manifest in her life with the power that God offered to her which she accepted. That night at church was a supernatural experience she will never forget. (We all must learn how to "wear" our new ornament, the new clothing God gives us.) The new wine skins have the new wine inside. We must take off the old wine skins and put on the new wine in our "new heart." Leaning not to our own understanding, but to the understanding that is of God. God will speak more when we listen.

Encounter at the Stairs

Church was out, and Linda was going downstairs to the restroom. As she reached the bottom step and stepped off, she met a friend. Susie, Linda's friend, approaches Linda with a strange look on her face, serious yet sad. She says, "I have to confess something to you." Linda was smiling to console her with a little joyful face. "Susie, what's the problem?"

They were always respectful and decent, and in the same church, not bosom buddies but casual friends. Susie had been a member of the church for some time. Susie had one son, he was six years old, and Linda had two children, her son was eight and her daughter was ten. The children all got along well.

"What could be the problem?" Susie says to Linda, "I have to tell you something." So, Linda moved a little beyond the steps downstairs, walks about an arm's length to the side of Susie, gives her a big smile and says, "Okay." Church was out, Linda was heading to the restroom before she headed home with the children. Their dad was out of town. Linda was in a bit of a hurry to get back home. Susie looked really serious, so Linda slowed down to let her speak or confess or share what seemed to be heavy on her heart. Then Susie laid down the bomb, she laid the bomb on Linda. A bomb that could potentially destroy Linda. Susie was not sure how the "bomb" would blow, evidently, she had thought it through. The church setting was a safe place. The timing was when Linda was professing a closer walk with God, surely, she would not go too crazy, maybe God would help her handle the information.

But at this point, six years for Susie, this burden was getting too much to bear. Susie had to tell someone to get it off her chest. So, Susie let it out. "I want to tell you that your children and my son are siblings." Linda asked, "What?" Susie was looking really serious and said, "Yes, they have the same dad." Linda stood still trying to process this situation. Susie had a baby by Linda's man.

Susie said, "When I met him, I did not realize he was your man at the club that night." Susie had not told anyone; this was a secret burden she had carried for six years, and the boy did not know his dad. Linda was in shock, not so much that her man cheated (he had cheated before) and but now when they were trying to mend their relationships, what will she do with this information?

Linda heard herself say, "Well if these kids are related by the same dad, we better let them know." Children need to know (the Holy Spirit would help her do the right thing). She heard herself say it is not fair for the children to suffer because of old folks' sins. She knew in her heart the truth could set the children and all involved free.

That night after church Linda told the children, "Susie's son is your brother." She let the children know it was news to her, too. "He's your dad's son. His mom told me today after church." Linda's daughter, age ten was more upset than her son, he was eight years old. Some friends at the church said it was good that the children learned at a younger age to accept the truth.

The truth is easier sometimes to accept at a younger age. Linda followed God's direction and accepted the truth. She believed the boy's mom Susie, as she had no reason to lie, and Linda saw clearly that the child looked like his dad. Linda was not married to her boyfriend, but they had been together over ten years. He did not have a permanent residence at her place, but they were trying to build a relationship where they would soon marry.

Linda confronted the situation with Jesus. God gave her the right way to comfort the children and help them to forgive and live in the midst of all the confusion. Children need both parents so Linda chose to stay in the picture. Her boyfriend confessed the affair and acknowledged the child as his own. Linda encouraged communication among the children with their dad. Linda and Susie kept their communication decent and in order at the church.

Thank God for Jesus and the power of the Holy Spirit. God is truly concerned about His people, not perfect but seeking to grow in Jesus. He gives power to the broken hearted and directions to the weak. The children grew up to appreciate and respect each other. Both moms encouraged communication with their dad. Both families were in church and able to manage the situation. (God will manage the hearts and minds of people when we let Him).

The sacrifice of praise: It is better to live in peace and love than to live in bitterness and hate. God can work out the good in all things when we let Him. Only God gives life. Abundant life comes from God. Living right is a sacrifice of praise. Praise God.

Remembering the Foreign Young Missionary from Africa

It was years ago, and Linda must have been ten or twelve. She followed her mom to church all the time. There were going to be a church service that night at her mom's church. This was a special evening service. It seems one of the missionaries was back from her missionary journey in Africa. Their church was a part of an organization that contributed to this particular mission with funds. Periodically, the missionary would come back to the USA to give a report on their missionary journeys, and share how the lord has blessed and provided for the people in the foreign country. They would give a report of the goodness of God and how their contributions had helped to supply and support the love in a foreign land.

This night service was to be very special. The missionary, an older black woman, would bring movies to show on a screen to see all the work of the missionary and the people of that community who were served in the foreign. The charity of the churches provided many health and food benefits to the poor people in the African towns. The movies on the big screen were very interesting, and Linda was very interested and glad her church was helping poor people in a foreign land in Africa.

The most interesting thing to Linda was the missionary, the tall women was black, and she had bought to the church one of the orphan children from the land of Africa with her to present the information. The girl was about fourteen years old, not much older than Linda, she was not very tall, medium dark with straight black hair. Linda found out later that she was Korean and African.

She helped the missionary explain the scenes and information and clarified the pictures on the movie screens. Periodically, she would speak in her own foreign language to the missionary, and she understood. The missionary was America, but she was also able to understand the native language of the young girl. This fascinated Linda, this young girl was dark like the speaker, and she was from a foreign land and had two languages. She could speak English and a foreign language also.

This was very interesting Linda to see the people of another country on the movie screen who loved the Lord just like Linda and her mom's church (they say the apple does not fall too far from the same tree). Later in life, Linda herself would become a missionary by sending her own money to an organization that would serve foreign lands she would contribute through the church and the foreign missions in the same way.

After the church service and the presentations, they served refreshments and Linda had an opportunity to talk to the young African girl. She shares with Linda some things and Linda asked for a foreign language sentence to remember. She gave Linda a sentence in her native tongue. Wa-ta-see-wa, I-not-a-hoe, I, E, she, ma, sue. Later Linda found out this was a formal version of I love you, a Korean sentence. It seems the African girl was Korean and African.

Her hair was cold-black and straight as a pin, and her skin was dark brown like Linda. Linda repeated the foreign sentence. Wa-tu-she-wa, I-not-a-hoe, I, E, she, ma, sue. Linda repeated it all the way back home in the car. Linda said to herself, now I have a friend in Africa, and I will never forget this foreign sentence she gave me. Wa-ta-see-wa, I-not-a-hoe, I, E, She, ma, sue. That night when Linda went to bed she said her foreign sentence and asked God to never let her forget her friend who taught her a foreign language.

As Linda went off to sleep, she said in her heart, I wish I knew a foreign language. She dreamed that she could speak a new foreign language. Linda never forgot that one sentence she learned at the age of twelve from the young African missionary girl who came to her mom's church and showed the movies of the African town.

Linda never saw those people again, but she never forgot the sentence spoken.. Wa-ta-see-wa, I-not-a-hoe, I, E, She, ma, sue. Linda tried the language on a few American Japanese people to see if they understood it. True enough, they said it was the Korean version of I love you (formal addition). Linda never remembered the bible missionary's name, but she never forgot the foreign language sentence, I love you.

I love you is such a universal language. God is love, and love is a word we will find in some form in every language and in every country. The word love comes from God, God is love.

L - Lord
O - Our
V - Victory
E - Eternal

In you

Coming Back Home

Linda came back to her home church. Linda was hesitant to leave her church when she got married but she asked the Lord and He said it is a good idea to go with your husband to his church. The Lord confirmed to Linda (the Lord usually gave Linda confirmations, visions, and information that was supernatural) by dreams. Linda saw in her dream a meeting of people and the pastor dressed in white was teaching the lesson and when he stood up at the head of the table, "a voice" spoke above him and said, "He is a great teacher."

And everyone sitting around the table made gesture that agreed with the "voice" that spoke above that pastor head in the dream. That's when Linda decided to go to that church. The interpretation of the dream to Linda was that if she decided to go to that church with her husband, she would learn much from this man of God the pastor and that it would be beneficial to her. So, she agreed to go and join her husband's church.

God confirmed it would benefit her knowledge and understanding about the Lord. Linda stayed at the church for nineteen years through the storms and the rains and all the hurricanes. Linda stayed in Bible School and dealt with all the situations and kept her faith in God, graduated and worked with the evangelist board as a member. The Bishop favored Linda as a daughter, and she knew he wanted her to remain at the church. Linda had asked God several times and God had not released her to return to her home church. She had stayed with the new pastor. He and his wife were still pastors and Linda was anxious to go home to her home church.

God knew Linda would have to be prepared for boot camp. After all, Linda was different now. She had grown shortly after receiving the baptism of the Holy Spirit, it was only a year later that she got married and left her home church. She understood now what had happened to her, the supernatural experiences, seeing the invisible, and feeling the intangible and the supernatural experience of speaking in unknown tongue that only God gives. Yes, Linda was different returning to her home church with a master's degree in Bible study, an ability to preach the Gospel with the anointing of the Holy Spirit, and more secure in faith in God and her relationship with the Lord; having conquered many natural storms, she was strong in her decision to follow Jesus.

Linda planned to be humble and not push for opportunities to speak or bring lectures or messages. Her pastor received her back to her church with open arms. He seemed proud that she had finished the Bible Theology College and congratulated her for her faithfulness and her decision to stay with God even though she was divorced now and her husband had remarried. Her pastor was so happy she was back at her home church.

He and his wife treated her with lots of love. But there was no mention as to how she could be a support to the church in leadership or how her pastor would allow her to use her gifts from the Lord. He did not ask Linda or even mention any leadership position he would like for her to operate in as a member of the church or where she could help him in his endeavor to evangelize the community. Linda did not push and quietly became a bench member with faithful attendance.

Back at the church, she felt good. Her pastor was such a fabulous preacher, and he knew the word and he preached the full gospel, and tt was under his ministry that she revealed the Baptism in the Holy Spirit. But it was clear he was not interested in Linda preaching or bringing a message to the congregation at all. Traditionally in the Baptist church, women did not preach in those days and he was not the one to be the tradition-changer (through the Bible tells us Mary Magdalene was the first women Jesus sent to tell the disciples He had risen). No problem, some people will know but they do not promote. Linda did not push the issue, in obedience to the Spirit of God.

She started a women's bible study at a popular restaurant at the mall. She and a few of her friends met on the third Saturday each month for lunch and a bible study. They were all working women. It was established that God wants us to be winners in every workplace we encounter, as wives and mothers, in our secular jobs as well as in the church. Several women from many churches started to meet together, the word was out. Lunch every third Saturday with Minister Linda and the restaurant manager was kind. After such an overwhelming success, (sometimes thirty to forty women) and given the banquet room at the restaurant, it all worked out.

The ladies ordered and purchased their own lunch, ordered in advance, and were served a short lesson. The manager of the restaurant looked for the group each month. He gave no charge for the private area in the restaurant. The group met for five years. Some months after the beginning, Linda felt lead to tell her pastor about how her outreach ministry was doing (no doubt he had already heard). Linda shared with her pastor about the women's bible class she had started, and he was glad to hear that she was using her gifts that God had given in her ability to teach the Gospel.

Linda further shared, "Anytime you want me to bring a lesson or share with the church, I am available." He was very patronizing and stated, "Linda that's great, you just keep doing what you are doing." So that is what Linda did as a trained missionary and a bible school graduate. Linda just bloomed wherever she was planted. The community of women in other churches began to call for Linda to speak and teach at church their programs and conferences. Linda honored her pastor with the invite information, and he always sent her off with his blessings. But she was not invited to speak at her own church. Linda was humble and obedient to the wishes of her pastor.

It was not until his own daughter confessed that she was called to the ministry that he softened his beliefs about women preachers. And he confessed to the whole congregation of his bias. So, thank God he was set free, and he began to invite Linda and his own daughter to preach in his pulpit.

The Bible certainly is true. Wait on the Lord, the Lord will make room for the gifts He has given you. Let God make the room, not you; when God makes the room, the room will be anointed. God wants us to wait on "his room, his opportunities, his space." He opens doors that no man can close, and He closes doors that no man can open.

The traditions of men can hinder the growth of the church. Search the scriptures then live in them, not according to the traditions of men. Then God gets all the Glory. The Bible Group evolved into an annual free women's conference each year with several community participants.

Liquid Love

Fill up on Liquid love, grow in power and purpose. Refuse to die in your spirit, but live and declare the works of the Lord in your life. Draw near to God and HE will draw near to you. Linda said, "Lord I do not want to just be a fake fruit centerpiece for the devil. No life, no breath, no Holy Ghost, no rest, just sitting and fading. Blending in, a movie star playing a part, but not Holy, not seeking, not searching how to grow in the Grace and in your knowledge. Jesus said seek after His word and you shall find. Knock and His door will be opened unto you."

Linda said, "Lord, protect my eye gate, protect my ear gate, and my touch gate. Lord, show me how to guard my heart because out of it flows the issue of life. Jesus, teach me your word. Just the fact your love is true, whether I believe it or not. Jesus, you sacrificed your life for me and became sin for me on the cross and if I believe and receive that fact, you will give me total forgiveness and adopt me into your Holy family. Even as I grow and become more like you Jesus, you will never forsake me or leave me, but I always have free will."

Linda said, "You have many blessings and gifts for me that I have not opened yet. Teach me all your promises from the will (the Bible) you left on record for me to read. Let me be your bride Jesus (the body of Christ). Lord, you show me how to break up with fear and connect with Faith."

Power Study

Linda learned the power study, she learned that her supernatural experience with God was another opportunity available to all. A power baptism available to the saved ones, according to Romans 10:9. Whoever desires the power baptism, God will give to him.

Christ came in human form to live like a human being. He was born by immaculate conception into human life. By the seed of a woman and the Holy Spirit, a supernatural seed birth came in the womb of Mary the mother of Jesus. Jesus was born and the Holy Spirit was His earth birth father. There was a plan to restore the human fellowship with Him. A blood sacrifice would deliver man from the penalty of sin to pay the price and to justify many.

It was at the cross where all debts were paid, and all sins were forgiven. Grace erases the penalty of sins committed on Earth, God forgives but the consequences of sin are real, and the Earth realm gives a penalty. But God forgives all sin by the blood of Jesus. Jesus rose from the natural death; His resurrection gives all opportunity to rise again with Him at the appointed time and he allows his children to influence the world for his kingdom to come.

Linda had the urgency to spread the good news. She had the desire to influence the world for the kingdom of God. She decided to put together a group of women. Several women would meet with her once a month at a restaurant to discuss and study the Bible for thirty minutes and then have lunch. It was a powerful group on the lunch hour, and at work, sometimes the women would come for a little prayer when needed it to strengthen them and to soften the stresses on the job, in our homes, and in the marketplace, letting their light shine for God to gets the Glory.

Being a light in the community came together from a force of women who would pray, encourage each other, and prepare for purposeful power in Jesus Christ. They were an infantry of prayed up, powerful women of God. A patient, pleasing, and prepared pretty group of women with a message of Christ. They were speakers, preachers, mothers, sisters, and daughters all who have a desire to grow in grace, knowledge, and skills to promote excellence.

THE IDENTITY
She Identified the Situation
A Spiritual Operation

She was leaving a church service-the preached word has gone forth, it was a woman's convention in Atlanta at a sports arena. The place was packed out, 65,000 women in one place at one time. It was a three-day conference, which was supposed to be a spiritual refresher and spiritual renewal opportunity, a little vacation as well. Women came from all over the United States to hear some famous preachers preach and teach about how to develop and grow in the grace and knowledge of God.

Linda and her friends are going up the escalator and there was a woman laying on the pavement nearby, she had three women standing over her looking perplexed not sure why she had "fainted" or fell out. They had observed already in the arena how several people had "fallen out" at the end of the service when the preacher, had given the last prayer over the entire audience (of the packed-out arena in Atlanta) He said, "no problem, some are slayed in the spirit of the Holy Spirit." When they fell into their seats, well Linda understood that feeling of being drunk in the spirit-because it happened to her.

Linda went over to the four women and she said, "no problem, your friend will be ok (the one on the pavement) she is just experiencing a Spiritual Operation." Linda heard herself say "Spiritual Operation" (wow she had never said that before). Her friends said great, then she will be okay, and Linda and her friends proceeded up the outside escalator of the Arena. Linda pondered this in her heart-God gave her the explanation. God told her what to say, "spiritual operation." She kept this definition in her heart.

Growing Salvation-A Spiritual Operation

For so long I had heard grow in grace and knowledge in Jesus Christ. I did not know until later that people really can grow spiritually, learn more, and trust more, and have an individual, personal intimate relationship with God, by His son Jesus Christ. We grow by the word of God, the more we read the Bible and seek to know the true and living God the more He will reveal to our Spirit, the more we understand the Bible and how to apply it to our lives, and how the love of Jesus works.

His love is unconditional-the more we accept his love, the more we will obey his word and seek his directions in everything we do. We will make mistakes which He will allow, because He wants us to love him on purpose. He loves us when we are right, and God loves us when we are wrong. The more we talk to God and read His will, the Bible, the easier it is to seek His face and trust Him, Jesus Christ teaches our spirit to be strong in the Lord.

Our flesh, fleshly desires want to take over and rule the natural body, so we must eat the word of God regularly by keeping His word in our mind and heart continually. Feed your spirit as you confer the word of God daily. In all you do-do for the glory of God. Accept Jesus Christ as your personal savior-quote the scriptures-meditate on the word of God.

Surrender to the word of God-recognize you cannot live by the media, popular opinions, or what everyone else is doing. After you surrender in your heart to Jesus Christ as your personal savior. He is your Lord, and He wants you to get to know Him in a special and personal relationship. He has a purpose for you. He wants you to be a witness for Him to bring others into the family of God. And teach others the love of God. He wants you to love the Lord with all your heart, mind, and soul. Accept the spiritual operations as you study God's word and grow in His unmerited favor. Favor comes from God. He loves all His children who will accept His son Jesus Christ. God sent His only son to sacrifice His life on the cross to pay for the sins of the word according to the scripture, that whosoever would believe in Him will have everlasting life. He became the blood sacrifice for the whole world.

Our Blood Sacrifice

He died and He rose again. God brought His son back. Jesus laid down His life for all the world. All sins are forgiven when you surrender your life to Christ. Surrender according to Romans 10:9. Say: "Yes, I am a sinner." "Yes, I need a savior." "Yes, I accept Jesus Christ, God's son as my personal savior." "I repent, Jesus come into my heart and help me grow in our relationship, salvation come now."

The Holy Spirit, the spirit of God, has now touched your natural spirit and invited and received you into the family of God, the Body of Christ. You are right now in the family of God, the body of Christ. Now God wants you to make a declaration to the Word. "I am saved." You do this by being baptized in natural water by a member of the body of Christ, the church, or the preacher. By this, you declare to the world, "I am saved." Saved from hell and saved to Heaven to you Lord and savior Jesus Christ. It is the only way to get to the true and living God, only by Him. Jesus Christ is the bridge to the father.

Accept His sacrifice on the cross and His blood covenant. Now safely covered by the protection of the blood of Jesus, the blood of Jesus covers you to go freely to our father in Heaven. Now we must eat the word of God so we can grow in His grace and knowledge and receive the fruits of the spirit- love, joy, peace, self-temperance, and long suffering. Man cannot live by bread alone but by every word that proceeds out of the mouth of God. The seed of the scripture will operate on your heart and mind and you will continue to grow in relationship with God. What you plant in your heart is what you will grow.

The spiritual operation has begun. Tell Jesus, "Yes Lord, yes Lord, to your will and to your way." Trust God. Learn and depend on Jesus. Read and know all the promises of God. Pray every prayer "in Jesus' name." Ask Jesus to lead and guide you and in everything acknowledge Him. Acknowledge Him. Grow your spirit up in Jesu; -feed your spirit and starve your doubt. Read the promises and no weapon formed against you will prosper. Water the word of God in your heart with what Jesus said. Eat well, grow in the power and in the strength to be a witness for Jesus Christ.

Man is…made of flesh, soul, spirit, three parts:

- Flesh-natural instincts
- Soul-appetite/desires
- Spirit-things of God(mind)

A Holy Spirit operation will keep your heart and mind in perfect peace.

Holy Spirit Operation=an operation on the spirit of man Salvation

Sanctification Phases of your future in Christ-spiritual continued operations Regeneration

All a Holy Spirit Operation. The Baptism in the Holy Spirit is another experience available to the body of Christ as well. I will speak on the experience later as well where the evidence is "speaking in tongues" and other gifts.

Notes to Remember

The Holy Spirit is our supernatural teacher. He is our comforter from Jesus Christ, sent to every believer to be an advocate of the Word of God. He does not speak of Himself. He only speaks of Jesus Christ.

The wealth of wisdom comes from God.

The weapons of our warfare are not fleshly but spiritual in power in the Holy Ghost.

Our security is our faith in God. Trust Him in all you do, Jesus is God, and He will lead your path as you grow in His unmerited favor (grace).

Appendix

Keys to Prosper and Have Good Success

- *Presence of God in your life
- Deut. 9:29
- II Kings 18:7
- 3 John
- *Walk in Obedience-key to His presence
- *Faith-Belief in the Bible
- Faith produces obedience
- *Hearing the Word of God (Scriptures Romans 10:17

These produce an incorruptible seed (a seed that will not spoil) in your spirit, the human spirit. In the incorruptible seed is the Word of God. The supernatural seed of God's son. Jesus Christ planted in the human will produce a supernatural operation to heal a sin-sick soul. Salvation is free, but not cheap.

Appendix

- What is the Christian Decision?
- <u>A Decision to Accept and Surrender to God</u>
- How does one become a part of the body of Christ?
- <u>The Christian church.</u>
- Can you buy a position in the Body of Christ?
- <u>The answer is no.</u>
- Can you earn a position in the Body of Christ if you do good works?
- <u>The answer is no.</u>
- Do your parents have to be good people?
- <u>The answer is no.</u>
- Do you need a college degree to get in?
- <u>The answer is no.</u>
- The question many still ask is: How do I get into the Body of Christ?
- <u>Easy-it's a Heart Entrance.</u>

Just accept Jesus Christ as your personal savior, it's a heart entrance.

- *Accept His death.*
- *Accept His burial.*
- *Accept His resurrection.*

You enter in by belief, Jesus reads your heart, and you confess with your mouth. (Romans 10:9)

- Just accept that you are a sinner in need of a Savior. (everyone needs a savior)
- We were all born in sin and shaped in iniquity. (Our born-again experience happens after natural birth). We are old enough to accept Jesus as personal Savior.
- Accept that apart from God and His Son Jesus Christ, you are lost when left to your own ability and self-will.
- Accept that God sent His only begotten Son, that whosoever belief in Him would not perish, but have everlasting life. (John 3:16)
- Accept the blood sacrifice of Jesus Christ on the cross as your bridge to God.
- Accept the immaculate conception of Jesus Christ.
- The Spirit of God overshadowed Mary, and Mary, a human woman, carried a Holy child, planted by God the Father.
- Accept the fact that Jesus Christ was born like a human being-an earthly man with a divine purpose.
- He, God, was wrapped in human flesh. (Luke 1:32-35)

The Son of God, Jesus Christ, was born into the world to become the human sacrifice for all the sins of the world.

We enter the Body of Christ with our heart, according to Romans 10:9. Confess with your mouth and believe in your heart that God has raised Jesus from the dead and you become saved, a member of the Body of Christ, your adoption is all done in the heart of man. For with the heart, one believes unto righteousness and with the mouth, confession is made unto salvation. (Romans 10:10)

The Body of Christ you are now adopted into the invisible church. The ordinance of the Holy Church requires that the candidate (just entered the invisible church) be baptized by faith into the earthly water (called baptism) is an outward show to the earthly world that you now belong to the body of Christ, the family of God. Water baptism, is a symbol that all your sins have been washed away and you are now under the blood of Jesus. All sins forgiven and grace is in the place of sin. The mercy of God is upon Jesus. For you and His goodness and mercy shall follow you all the days of your life.

Now you are in the body of Christ. Adopted, as a newborn baby, now you desire the milk of the Lord that you may grow thereby. Eat the word of God, drink the milk of the Bible, earth the word of God, and grow in the grace and in the knowledge of Jesus Christ. God wants a relationship with his people. We have an advocate with the Father because of Jesus Christ.

The only way to get to the Father is by Jesus Christ, a Holy Ghost invitation. Accept Him as personal savior and as you grow, He will give you many spiritual gifts. No longer guilty, now your record is clean. Now your heart is pure. You are righteous under the blood of Jesus. The new covenant is in your heart. Jesus is the new covenant, you are no longer under the law of Moses.

Sinful man has no strength to follow the ten commandments apart from God. They tried and found out the "flesh" has its own agenda. Man cannot live righteous when left to himself.

But God sent His Son to give man opportunity to be covered by the blood of Jesus. He put blood on the doorpost of our hearts, so that the death angel would pass over our sins and God's grace, (his unmerited favor) would keep us, the body of Christ safe under the blood of Jesus. Isaiah 53 prophesied our blood sacrifice, Jesus. He was wounded for our transgression (sins), and He was bruised for our iniquities (our hatred, unforgiving bitterness, prejudices, and evilness).

Jesus was chastised (beaten) that we might have peace (they beat Him bloody from head to toe). Our peace had been paid for, our peace is found under the blood of Jesus, and our peace has been purchased. Jesus paid the price for the human condition of man. The price of death on the cross, Jesus, our blood sacrifice, redeemed mankind back to God. He accepted the penalty allowed by His Father God.

It pleased the Lord to bruise Him. God made His soul an offer for sin. Jesus died and was buried in a borrowed tomb (Joseph's tomb). God brought His son out of the grave three days later. (Isaiah 53:10) Jesus is risen. (Luke 24:1-7) He had promised that He would rise on the third day. Jesus Christ came back from the dead and spoke to many people. (Luke 24:13) He spoke to His disciples. (Luke 24:36-43, Luke 24:28-35)

He was beat with many stripes and by each stripe, each lash of the leather whip on his skin was the healing of the nation for those who would believe. Imagine the beatings. The whip was made up of long pieces of leather strips with nails and razors attached to cut the skin with each lash. Each whip had several long leather petals of razors and nail prongs. The stripes were a sacrifice for every healing needed in the world and human condition. Jesus paid it all. He can give us:

- Healing of the mind- the control center operation in man.
- Healing of the body- the flesh, the physical man.
- Healing of the soul- where desires, appetite, and passions reside in man.

Who will believe the report? Those who believe the report are healed, saved, and delivered. The Scripture Isaiah 53 asks the question of the report to come (a prophecy of Jesus). Jesus told His disciples that He had risen, but He must go away to His Father. After so many days with them, He left.

Jesus said: I must go prepare a place for you, that where I am, you may be also. But Jesus said He would send a comforter. He said the comforter will come when I go. He will keep you, the Holy Spirit, the comforter, will teach you all things whatsoever I have told you. Jesus sent the comfort of the Holy Spirit. He is here today. He comforts the believer. He teaches and speaks to the believer on behalf of Jesus Christ. He is the third person of the Trinity (the Holy Spirit).

- *The Father*
- *The Son*
- *The Holy Spirit*

You get into the body of Christ, you come into the body of Christ when you accept Jesus as personal savior, by belief and faith. The only way to the true and living God is by way of the Jesus Christ, none can come to the Father (God) except by the son Jesus Christ.

The Three Baptisms offered to the World from God

- Baptized into the body of Christ
  To accept and surrender to the Bible believe the report, (performed by the Holy Spirit)

- Baptized in Water (natural water)
  To demonstrate your new inward birth as a show to the world- you are now born again by the Spirit of God (performed by the preacher)

- Baptized into the Holy Spirit
  A supernatural baptism another experience (performed by Jesus Christ) after salvation- must surrender, a baptism into power. A Holy Spirit power for service in the leadership of God's business, an increase in the gifts of God.

Change Your Life with One Prayer

Heavenly Father, Dear God I accept Jesus Christ, your Son as my personal savior. I believe He sacrificed His life for mine on the cross. You sent your only begotten Son that whoever would believe in Him would be saved and have eternal life. I repent of my sins and I invite you Jesus to come into my heart and become my personal savior and Lord. Thank you for saving me according to the Bible. (Romans 10:9)

Now that I am baptized into the body of Christ, your supernatural Church, now I want to join a physical church in the neighborhood where I can grow in the grace and knowledge of my Lord and savior Jesus Christ. Teach me your ways, Lord.

Signed__________________________________

A life surrendered to the work of Jesus Christ

Life Application

A saved person is one who has been set right with God, adopted into the divine family, and now dedicated to the service of the Lord. This salvation is Free. This person is made righteous on the confession of their faith in Jesus Christ as personal savior. According to I John 1:12, to as many as believe, God gave them power to become the "sons of God." The Book of St. John is a great book to read to introduce you to Jesus- the human man and the Christ- our sacrifice on the cross- Jesus Christ and His life plan for you.